RENAISSANCE
PAPERS
1975

RENAISSANCE
PAPERS
1975

Editors

DENNIS G. DONOVAN

A. LEIGH DENEEF

Published by
THE SOUTHEASTERN RENAISSANCE CONFERENCE
1976

THE SOUTHEASTERN RENAISSANCE CONFERENCE

Renaissance Papers 1975
All rights reserved
Library of Congress Catalog Card Number A 55-3551
Editorial Office
402 Allen Building, Duke University
Durham, North Carolina 27706

Printed in Spain
for the Southeastern Renaissance Conference by
Artes Gráficas Soler, S. A. - Jávea, 28 - Valencia 8

I.S.B.N.: 84-399-4550-7
Depósito Legal: V. 3.471 - 1975

TABLE OF CONTENTS

Renaissance Papers

A Selection of Papers
presented at the
Thirty-second Annual Meeting
April 25-26, 1975
The Virginia Military Institute
Lexington, Virginia

The Dialectic of Genres in
The Shepheardes Calender

IN A RECENT STUDY of the Renaissance pastoral tradition, Patrick Cullen demonstrates a basic dialectical structure in *The Shepheardes Calender.*[1] Beginning with the assumption that the pastoral evaluates experience by juxtaposing different perspectives, Cullen argues that Spenser dramatizes his *Calender* by placing a pagan, Arcadian viewpoint in confrontation with a Christian, Mantuan one. In each individual eclogue, this dramatic confrontation underlies the more obvious debates: youth versus age, spring versus winter, the active life versus the contemplative life, the hills versus the dales, and so forth. Rendered in schematic fashion, Cullen's argument "unfolds" the central Arcadian-Mantuan opposition into the following terms. The Arcadian perspective "signifies," among other things, spring, youth, the high estate, passion, confidence in the world, participation, ambition, and a celebratory tone. Its speakers are Cuddie, Willie, Palinode, Morrell, and Hobbinol. The Mantuan perspective "signifies" winter, old age, the low estate, reason, *contemptus mundi,* withdrawal, disillusionment, and an elegiac tone. Its speakers are Thenot, Thomalin, Piers, Colin, and Diggon Davie.

The importance of Cullen's reading is that it alters fundamentally the more typical view of the *Calender* as a unity into which Spenser crams the greatest possible multeity. It suggests that the variety of metrics, characters, and motifs functions within the *Calender* in more precise structural ways than usually assumed. For one thing, Cullen's view allows us to see the drama of the individual eclogues as mirroring those larger dialectical issues which concern Spenser in

---

[1] *Spenser, Marvell, and Renaissance Pastoral* (Cambridge: Harvard U.P., 1970).

the whole (indeed throughout all his poetic wholes): cyclic time versus linear time, providence versus fortune, spiritual immortality versus seasonal rebirth. Even more important, it allows us to see a central dialectic between poetic voices: between, that is, the poet who fails to resolve the argumentative dialogues, or who perversely binds himself to the linear and destructive progression of the year — Colin Clout — and the poet who accommodates both sides of all the debates and whose song finally orders the disparate perspectives into one unified vision — Spenser himself. [2] By consistently aligning Colin with the wintery, withdrawing, disillusioned view of experience, Spenser sets him in dramatic opposition to his own voice and thereby clarifies his own poetic achievement, his own constructed song.

What I would like to propose here is that this dialectical structure extends beyond the motifs of the individual eclogues or the voices of the different shepherds to a dialectic of poetic genres as well. As S. K. Heninger and others have argued, Spenser's ultimate vision in *The Shepheardes Calender* is a *formal* one. [3] Heninger, for instance,

---

[2] Cullen is one of the few critics to read Colin as an exemplum of a poet who fails, but even he does not go far enough. Compare the more typical view of Colin, here described by A. C. Hamilton:

> The ritual quest for God becomes the quest for himself, and the poem's major theme is the effort [of Colin] to "find" himself. The association of the Calendar with the Nativity adds the life-death-life sequence, and the mutability of life that brings death within nature is opposed at the end of the poem by the November eclogue where for the first time the pagan mood of despair is supplanted by the full Christian assurance of man's resurrection out of Nature. This assurance, together with the aspiration in October to cast off his shepherd's weeds, brings him [Colin] to the resolution of the final eclogue when he lays down the oaten pipe and emerges as England's heroic poet.

("The Argument of Spenser's *Shepheardes Calender*," in *Spenser*, ed. Harry Berger [Englewood Cliffs: Prentice-Hall, 1968], p. 33). My major argument with Hamilton's view is that the aspiration of October is not Colin's at all, nor is it even Cuddie's, but an exhortation on the part of Piers. As Cuddie tells us, Colin *might* aspire, "were he not with love so ill bedight." But he *is* "so ill bedight," and nowhere in the poem does he suggest that he lays his pipe aside to sing some greater song. See James N. Brown, " 'Hence with the Nightingale Will I Take Part': A Virgilian Orphic Allusion in Spenser's 'Avgvst'," *Thoth* 13 (1972-73): 13-18, who argues that Colin is a "type" of the *failed* Orpheus; and John W. Moore, Jr., "Colin Breaks His Pipe: A Reading of the 'January' Eclogue," *ELR* 5(1975): 3-24.

[3] "The Implications of Form for *The Shepheardes Calender*," *SR* 9(1962): 309-21. My indebtedness to Heninger's conceptions of form should be obvious.

2

aligns it with conventional Renaissance notions of *concordia discors,* but he does not go on to suggest how that conception affects Spenser's use of literary genres. With Cullen's work before us, however, we can better understand why Spenser does not resolve the thematic and generic oppositions within the *Calender;* instead, he creates a perceptual *frame* which contains, orders, and fixes them. As frequently happens in *The Faerie Queene,* differing perspectives are not ultimately judged as right or wrong, but transformed into a concord literally based upon, indeed *dependent upon and growing out of,* elements of obvious discord. In this transformation, Spenser's dialectic of the genres themselves is centrally important in directing the reader to his final subsuming vision.

Let me begin with some obvious thematic oppositions in order to suggest how the generic ones function. Many readers of the *Calender* have recognized that the April eclogue on Elisa and the November one on Dido are dramatic "centers" of the work as a whole. Both represent moments in which the linear progression of time through the year is transcended. In April, Spenser moves backwards in time in order to recreate Elisa as the mythic spring-goddess of fertility and regeneration. As the Fourth Grace, Elisa stands as a permanent center, unchanged and unmoved, within the yearly cycle. Dido, recreated as a heavenly spirit, is similarly unchanging and unmoving. Both figures achieve eternity through a form of investiture: Elisa in the garb of Nature; Dido in that of the Spirit. But what is the relationship between them? If Elisa represents a natural, seasonal immortality and Dido a Christian one, are we to read them as dialectical opposites, as symbolic analogues, or as complementary aspects of the same continuum?

The answer to these questions is clear once we understand the *kind* of song Colin sings in the two eclogues. In April, he constructs a pastoral *blazon,* festive and optimistic, celebratory in tone. In November, he constructs a formal *dirge,* or *threnody,* elegiac and lamenting. Spenser exploits these two genres for their rhetorical opposition of compliment and complaint, but ultimately they are identical in effect. As epideictic instruments of praise, both songs transform or translate their subjects into a specifically *poetic* immortality which frames the pagan and Christian perspectives in a larger, subsuming vision made more complete by the presence of

3

both at once. The *blazon* and the *dirge* dilate, in other words, to the grander genre of the *hymn,* and this generic dialectic reveals the formal concord of Spenser's poetic vision.

In the February eclogue Spenser uses a similar generic opposition. As Cuddie and Thenot argue about the general winter-spring cycle of seasons, their argument takes the form of a conventional youth versus age *débat.* At the end of the eclogue, Thenot tells a *fable* about an oak and a briar to support his own perspective, but Cuddie dismisses it as a "lewd tale." As Cullen's thematic analysis suggests, Spenser does not present the *fable* as a simple parallel to the *debate,* for the oak and the briar serve as perverse and tragic extensions of Thenot and Cuddie. By setting the *débat* and the *fable* against one another, Spenser creates a *mixed* genre which subsumes the two arguments in a broader vision and which forces the reader to accommodate the narratively disparate perspectives.

As a third example, we might look briefly at the August eclogue. In the first half of the eclogue Perigot and Willye argue the "mischaunce" of love; in the second half, Cuddie sings of Colin's similar adventure. But again Spenser sets the two versions of "mischaunce" in dialectical opposition by heightening the rhetoric of their respective genres: the comic parody of Willye and Perigot's *song-contest* versus the "dooleful" seriousness of Colin's *planctus.* And, as in "February," Spenser's mixing of both genres within the same eclogue leads the reader to a subsuming, accommodating form.

This generic emphasis — from the limited or partial perspectives of individual genres set in opposition to other limited genres, to a larger *genus mixtum* whose concord is the result of the discord it frames — underlies the whole of *The Shepheardes Calender.* As we move through the various eclogues, Spenser invites us to question the generic "sets" which comprise those eclogues. He invites us, in other words, to anticipate certain motifs, attitudes and stances, even verbal textures, by focusing on clearly defined literary genres. Whether the genre be planctus, débat, fable, mock-epic, blazon, beast epic, encomium, song-contest, dirge, or lament, we understand

---

[4] I adopt the term from the recent studies of Rosalie Colie; see notes 5 and 9 below.

the themes of each eclogue by the generic forms through which those themes are explored. But by continuously shifting us from one genre to another, Spenser never allows us a point of fulfilled expectations. Each new genre radically alters the perspective(s) of the preceding one(s) and we are forced to keep readjusting our view of the whole in order to accommodate conflicting traditions. There is more to this movement than a simple desire for scope or variety. Even if we try to view the progression of genres in a sort of hierarchic ranking we are frustrated. Presumably, we could define the *pastoral* as the true genre of the work and interpret all other forms — blazon, contest, elegy — as sub-genres of that larger one. Although this reading has much to recommend it, the versions of pastoral which Spenser puts before us are still bewildering.

As Rosalie Colie and others have reminded us, the pastoral is not so much a genre as a mode embracing many particular genres. [5] The pastoral mode of Sidney's *Arcadia,* for example, allows the poet to display a wide variety of topical and formal genres. Indeed, from Guarini's *Il pastor fido* on, most Renaissance literary criticism assumed that the pastoral was *the* mixed generic form, and the persistent debate over such mixtures as tragi-comedy, whether pro or con, used the mixed mode of the pastoral as an official locus from which to argue. [6] Only the epic, from which, according to the literary theorists, all poetic genres evolved, competed with the pastoral as a universally accepted *genus mixtum.* This fact alone is revealing: might one of the impulses behind Spenser's obvious push toward the epic be the same generic one which led him originally to the pastoral?

We can clarify the generic issue by noting that two poets are consistently idealized in *The Shepheardes Calender,* one of them real and one mythic. The first is Chaucer, called Tityrus after and frequently aligned with, Virgil; the second is Orpheus. Spenser defines both "poets" in similar terms. In "February," Thenot describes the songs of Tityrus as follows:

[5] See especially, *Shakespeare's Living Art* (Princeton: Princeton U.P., 1974), Chapters 6 and 7; also, Donald M. Friedman, *Marvell's Pastoral Art* (Berkeley: U. California P., 1970).
[6] *Shakespeare's Living Art,* pp. 243-45.

> Many meete tales of youth did he make,
> And some of love, and some of chevalrie.
>
> (98-99) [7]

In "June" Colin laments:

> The god of shepheards, Tityrus, is dead,
> Who taught me, homely as I can, to make.
> He, whilst he lived, was the soveraigne head
> Of shepheards all that bene with love ytake:
> Well couth he wayle his woes, and lightly slake
> The flames which love within his heart had bredd,
> And tell us mery tales, to keepe us wake,
> The while our sheepe about us safely fedde.
>
> (81-88)

In "October" the "Romish" Tityrus is described by Cuddie as one who

> left his oaten reede,
> Whereon he earst had taught his flocks to feede,
> And laboured lands to yield the timely eare,
> And eft did sing of warres and deadly drede,
> So as the heavens did quake his verse to here.
>
> (56-60)

And finally, in "December," Spenser refers in passing to the songs (the plural is significant, since Colin is about to sing his typical monologue) Colin has learned from Tityrus.

The result of these descriptions is that Tityrus, as the arch-poet, represents a merging of poetic choices. He sings merry tales *and* lamentations, simple love songs *and* martial epics. E. K. directs us to this generic emphasis by glossing the lines from "October" quoted above:

> In these three verses are the three severall workes
> of Virgile intended. For in teaching his flocks to
> feed, is meant his *Æglogues.* In labouring of lands,
> is hys *Bucoliques.* In singing of wars and deadly
> dreade, is his divine *Æneis* figured.
>
> (119-24)

---

[7] All quotations are taken from *The Poems of Spenser,* ed. R. E. Neil Dodge (Boston: Houghton-Mifflin, 1908).

Tityrus stands, therefore, as a counterpoint to Colin, who now sings only one lamenting song, and he symbolizes the poetic combination of perspectives which Colin is unable to achieve. Pushed one step further, the references to Tityrus suggest that it is precisely his ability to combine generic perspectives that assures his fame and influence as a poet. This is one reason why ,Colin's January and December songs are identical lamenting *mono*logues: they do not combine discordant viewpoints but choose between opposing options. By that choice, Colin seals his death, both literally and poetically. Here, then, is a precise comment on the use of literary genres: by themselves, at their best and no matter how beautiful, they represent a distorted view of experience, distorted by the very limits which define the genre as a genre. Presumably, the true poet is he who is able to transcend the limited *sets* of individual genres, he who is able to construct ("make" in Colin's terms) a mixed form which will actualize all options at once.

Orpheus is mentioned only once in the *Calender,* but the reference occurs in the crucial poetic debate of "October":

> Soone as thou gynst to seete thy notes in frame,
> O how the rurall routes to thee doe cleave!
> Seemeth thou doest their soule of sense bereave,
> All as the shepheard, that did fetch his dame
> From Plutoes balefull bowre withouten leave:
> His musicks might the hellish hound did tame.
>
> (25-30)

The significance of this allusion lies in the notion of the opening lines: that of Cuddie *framing* individual notes into song. We recall E. K.'s epistle to the *Calender* in which he commends the poet for

> his dewe observing of decorum everye where, in personages, in seasons, in matter, in speach, and generally in al seemely simplycitie of handeling his matter, and framing his words.
>
> (28-32)

In a later passage, E. K. continues this praise:

> For what in most English wryters useth to be loose, and as it were ungyrt, in this authour is well

7

> grounded, finely framed, and strongly trussed up
> together.
>
> (167-71)

The idea of *framing* is repeatedly mentioned in the *Calender* (see
also "June," ll. 57, 78; "August," l. 3; among others), but for our
purposes the most important instance occurs in E. K.'s gloss on
the lines immediately preceding the Orpheus passage quoted above.
Explaining the Orphic origins of poetry, E. K. argues:

> some learned man, being more hable then the rest
> for speciall gyftes of wytte and musicke, would take
> upon him to sing fine verses to the people, in prayse
> eyther of vertue or of victory or of immortality, or
> such like. At whose wonderful gyft al men being
> astonied and as it were ravished with delight, think-
> ing (as it was indeed) that he was inspired from
> above, called him *vatem:* which kinde of men after-
> warde framing their verses to lighter musick (as of
> musick be many kinds, some sadder, some lighter,
> some martiall, some heroical: and so diversely eke
> affect the mynds of men) found out lighter matter
> of poesie also, some playing wyth love, some
> scorning at mens fashions, some powred out in
> pleasures: and so were called poetes or makers.
>
> ("October," gloss, 29-46)

Obviously, to E. K., *framing* is an intrinsically poetic gift, by which
specific subjects are *tuned* to appropriate forms, or *kinds*.

In the epilogue, Spenser himself alludes to his larger *frame* when
he writes:

> Loe! I have made a Calender for every yeare,
> That steele in strength, and time in durance, shall outweare:
> And if I marked well the starres revolution,
> It shall continewe till the worlds dissolution.
>
> (1-4)

The frame of the pastoral "Calender" is largely a generic conception
in these lines, a shaping force and form for the work as a whole. The
Calender, as the song by which the various opposing and discordant
notes are set in final harmony, is the poet's literary version of the
universal harmony of the spheres. Like that macrocosmic concord,

Spenser's poem is a *tuning* (we notice how frequently this image arises in descriptions of the songs within the *Calender*) of the various discords. E. K. once more underscores this point, although his professed subject is Spenser's language:

> (for oftimes we fynde our selves, I knowe not how, singularly delighted with the shewe of such naturall rudenesse, and take great pleasure in that disorderly order) even so doe those rough and harsh termes enlumine and make more clearly to appeare the brightnesse of brave and glorious words. So ofentimes a dischorde in musick maketh a comely concordaunce.
>
> (Epistle, 93-101)

As I have argued elsewhere, this particular view of poetry underlies Renaissance conceptions of the Orphic nature of *decorum*. [8] Decorum, proper framing, tuning, if you will, is a magical power derived from Orpheus by which the poet re-creates a sense of universal order and stability out of disorder and conflict. *The Shepheardes Calender,* therefore, as a particular mixed poetic form, subsumes and orders the conflicting generic sets dramatically opposing one another throughout and between the twelve eclogues, and in so doing it reaches out toward the universal.

To repeat an earlier point, the pastoral mode is essentially a critical one by which the poet tests the limits of differing perspectives on experience. Generically, the same testing obtains, with the same self-critical results. Each genre presents a limited and thus myopic point of view: it presupposes, indeed is defined by, set patterns, set approaches, set answers. By dramatically placing such myopic sets against one another in dialectical fashion, Spenser demonstrates his awareness of a given genre's inability to mirror the more complex experience it attempts to capture, and he literally creates out of their interplay the larger Orphic vision of which all genres are but refractions. Thus his use of genre is both thematic and formal, in each case pointing toward the calendric frame which *completes* the inadequacies of the individual genres which comprise

---

[8] See my "Epideictic Rhetoric and the Renaissance Lyric," *JMRS* 3(1973): 203-31, and a forthcoming monograph, *The Poetics of Orpheus: A Study and Text of "Orpheus His Journey to Hell."*

it. Truth, in *The Shepheardes Calender,* does not reside in a one-sided choice between opposing viewpoints, but the *pattern* which grows out of the dialectical opposing itself.

Renaissance poets were as aware as we are of the restrictive and arbitrary nature of genres. But they did not therefore discount genres as material for original or profound expression. In fact, the persistence with which they mixed and remixed generic elements is itself a testament to how fertile generic thinking was for them. We ought, then, to pay closer attention to the various ways in which genres are used dialectically to create new *genera mixta.* Still, we might ask, why mix genres at all? If it were simply a desire for originality we would dismiss the whole issue as an interesting but rather facile exercise. In Spenser's *Calender* a more compelling reason appears, for here the *genus mixtum* also reaches out toward the *genus universum.* [9] This attempt at totality is as persistent a Renaissance approach to genre as that of mixing. And in each instance, we can see the artist ultimately turning literary models back toward life itself, trying desperately to find a form to capture its contradictions and its mysteries. For all its high Renaissance artifice, *The Shepheardes Calender* demonstrates Spenser's broader concern with this issue. Unwilling on every level to accept simplistic answers to life's questions, Spenser continually forces his genres beyond their partial perspectives to a complex pattern reflecting the complexity of life itself. Ultimately, of course, even the pattern of the *Calender* as a whole proved unsatisfactory in these terms and Spenser was led to an even greater *genus mixtum, The Faerie Queene.* By returning to the epic, the form from which all genres evolved, Spenser tries once more to achieve the *genus universum.*

Duke University   A. LEIGH DENEEF

---

[9] I am again indebted to Colie for the conception of a *genus universum.* See, besides the work cited above, her *Resources of Kind* (Berkeley: U. California P., 1973). One might argue, of course, that in so far as a given poet accepts his art as inspired by Orpheus, he sees only one true genre: all commonly-defined "genres" are merely differing "angles" of the one Orphic *Vision,* the ultimate *genus universum.* Spenser's interest in totality, of course, is clear simply from the sheer range of literary *kinds* he includes within the *Calender.*

Leone Ebreo and Florentine Neoplatonism

L EONE EBREO HAS ALWAYS been assigned a special place in the line of Neoplatonic love philosophers that sprang from Marsilio Ficino. He was not a Florentine but a Jew of the distinguished family of Abravanel, a refugee from his native Portugal who brought with him a knowledge of Hebrew, Arab, and medieval Christian traditions. What he made of them is especially interesting to students of the English Renaissance, since Leone's writings were well known in Elizabethan England. [1]

The *Dialoghi D'Amore*, first published in 1535, but probably written some thirty years earlier, take the form of three long and sometimes lively conversations in Italian between a philosophical lover, Filone, and his reluctant but inquisitive beloved, Sofia. [2] Their subject is love, its nature, scope and origin. A promised fourth dialogue on the effects of love has not come down to us. Unlike Ficino's *De Amore*, which is a free commentary on the speeches of the *Symposium*, the *Dialoghi* follow a pattern of question, answer, objection,

---

[1] See Sears R. Jayne, "Ficino and the Platonism of the English Renaissance," *Comparative Literature*, 4 (1952), 231.

[2] Ed. Santino Caramella (Bari: Laterza, 1929); an English version is *The Philosophy of Love*, tr. F. Friedeberg-Seeley and Jean H. Barnes (London: Soncino Press, 1937). There is a monograph by Heinz Pflaum, *Die Idee der Liebe; Leone Ebreo* (Tübingen: Mohr, 1926). Carlo Dionisotti, "Appunti su Leone Ebreo," in *Italia Medioevale e Umanistica*, 2 (1959), 409-28, discusses the genesis and text of the work, saying that it was not originally Italian but was translated, perhaps from Hebrew. Others have suggested Spanish. These matters are discussed and a bibliography given in the edition of Caramella. A recent article by T. Anthony Perry, "Dialogue and Doctrine in Leone Ebreo's *Dialoghi d'Amore*," *PMLA*, 88 (1973), 1173-79, urges that the work be taken seriously as a dialogue in which Sofia's persistent questioning obliges Filone to modify and make explicit his own views. Perry rightly notes the scriptural origin of Leone's distinctive views.

11

and rejoinder, which combines the method of Socrates with that of the Schoolmen. Sofia is a relentless disputant, and few of Filone's arguments are left unquestioned. The result is a treatment of love more exacting than Ficino's, and, thanks to the humor of Filone's pose as the lovelorn philosopher, more entertaining.

Filone's straightforward declaration at the outset, "My acquaintance with you, Oh Sofia, awakens in me both love and desire," [3] sets in motion a long debate on the relationship between love and desire. At first Filone insists on distinguishing between the two; later in the *Dialoghi* he will admit that they are synonymous. But although he allows desire a place at the center of love, he does not understand love chiefly as a tendency toward the possession of an object. This becomes clear from his discussion of three kinds of love: *amore utile,* which is directed at useful things; *amore delettabile,* which is directed at things which give pleasure; and *amore onesto,* which is directed at what is virtuous. [4] Whereas in the first two instances, virtue lies in a mean, since excess of pain or of pleasure are extremes whence flow the worst of vices, "in respect of the good, the more excessive and unrestrained our love and desire, the more praiseworthy and virtuous it is." [5] This is because *amore onesto* is the love of spirit or intellect, which is the source of all good, whereas love of profit or pleasure is connected with matter, and so must be moderated by reason, lest the material element drag it down to the level of brute beasts. [6]

Virtuous love takes many forms: love of God, love of father for child, of master for servant, of husband for wife, and of friends for each other. Apart from divine love, love of friendship seems to be the most perfect embodiment of *amore onesto.* Leone's treatment of friendship, like Ficino's, owes much to Aristotle, and their dependence on a common source leads to certain common features. Both agree that the true friend is another self, and that those linked in friendship share a single being, and hence a single life and activity; they are one soul in bodies twain. But even here there is a difference.

[3] *Philosophy of Love,* p. 3; *Dialoghi,* p. 5.
[4] *Philosophy,* p. 12 ff.; *Dialoghi,* p. 13 ff.
[5] *Philosophy,* p. 23; *Dialoghi,* p. 23.
[6] *Philosophy,* pp. 25-26; *Dialoghi,* pp. 24-25.

Ficino, at least in the *De Amore*, praises mutual love above all as a wondrous exchange — *o mirum commercium!* — in which two lovers who surrender themselves not only regain their existence but double their gain in finding two lives instead of one. Leone stresses not reciprocal possession, but mutual sharing in union, "in which one love shall hold the hearts of both friends." [7] He also grounds the relationship ontologically by asserting that friendship is a union based on mutual virtue or wisdom, spiritual qualities which override bodily individuality and engender in friends *"una propria essenzia mentale"* which makes of the two persons one. [8] This stress on unity is also apparent in the first tentative definition of love which Filone offers Sofia in the course of their argument about love and desire. Love is "an affect of the will to enjoy through union the thing judged good." [9]

Leone departs still further from Ficino — and Pico, too — in the attention he pays to love between the sexes. The form of his work is significant; the *Dialoghi* are exchanges between a man and a woman, the first of whom professes a love both virtuous and passionate. Perfect love between the sexes is born of reason, that is to say, of a knowledge of the other's intelligence and beauty of mind and person. [10] Such a love begets a tendency or desire that the two may form but a single person. In order that union of bodies may correspond to union of spirits, love gives rise to a longing for physical union as well. When it is inspired by spiritual love, such desire is unlike that love of the pleasurable described above, which ceases upon possession. When desire is generated by love, what ceases is simply a particular desire for the physical acts of love; these, though intermittent, serve to support and strengthen, rather than dissolve genuine love between the sexes.

Still, Leone's praise of love between the sexes is not free of a certain hesitation. To begin with, in one place he classifies conjugal love as *amore delettabile*, though it shares in *amore onesto*. In the third dialogue he appears to backslide, writing that love which is materially pleasurable has little or no true goodness or beauty. To

---

[7] *Philosophy*, p. 31; *Dialoghi*, pp. 29-30.
[8] *Philosophy*, p. 31; *Dialoghi*, p. 30.
[9] *Philosophy*, p. 12; *Dialoghi*, p. 13.
[10] *Philosophy*, p. 57; *Dialoghi*, p. 52.

Sofia's objection that such pleasures are clearly intended by nature, Filone answers that carnal pleasures are indeed virtuous, but they receive their formal virtue only from their moderate use and not from their material nature. For virtuous love is formally only of the intellect, as indeed perfection itself is intellectual. [11] Although more "incarnational" in this respect than is the Christian Ficino, Leone Ebreo never abandons the Platonic assumption that value is of the spirit, and shared by material beings only extrinsically thanks to their association with spiritual beings.

Leone's idea of love seems more "Christian" than Ficino's in still another way. To Ficino the boundless aspiration of the lover is perfectly reasonable, since he is trying to become a God instead of a man; and who would not exchange the human condition for the divine? Leone holds that, although love is begotten of reason, that is to say, of a recognition of the other's virtue, once born it no longer submits to the rule and order of reason which bore it. "For he who truly loves another unloves himself; which is against all reason and duty. For love is charity, and should begin at home; but we disregard this, loving others more than ourselves: a noteworthy thing!" [12] Perfect dedication leads the lover to endure suffering and even death. It cannot be bound by ordinary reason, whose purpose is to sustain and preserve man in the good life. Brotherly love is guided by an extraordinary reason which takes no care to safeguard its own interests, but prefers instead the possession of the beloved, even as the best is to be preferred before the good. [13] Leone even accounts for the traditional symptoms of the distracted lover, which Ficino had attributed to *amor vulgaris,* by this notion of supra-rational love. [14]

Divine love is also seen in a different light. The love of God is of course the greatest of all, since it "not only partakes of good, but comprises the goodness of all things and all loves; for the Godhead is at once the origin, means and end of all good deeds." [15] Such love is always united with desire, a desire to attain whatever we lack

---

11 *Philosophy,* pp. 436-38; *Dialoghi,* pp. 365-67.
12 *Philosophy,* p. 58; *Dialoghi,* pp. 52-53.
13 *Philosophy,* p. 63; *Dialoghi,* pp. 57-58.
14 *Philosophy,* p. 60; *Dialoghi,* pp. 54-55.
15 *Philosophy,* p. 31; *Dialoghi,* p. 30.

in knowledge of God; [16] but the act of loving God is not as such the final end of human existence. To be sure, fulfillment consists in the attainment of the One in whom all good is present. But He is attained in an act of the intellect — not in the first act of knowing God, which must precede love, nor in the love which draws us toward union with the object of that knowledge, but in the act of cognitive union with God. In such union lies the final perfection of created minds. The term of our aspiration is neither knowledge nor love, but the union which is achieved in loving knowledge. Such a state "transcends the limits of human capacity and speculation, and attains to such union and copulation with God Most High, as proves our intellect to be, rather a part of the essence of God, than understanding of merely human form." [17] Does God reciprocate our love? Plato cannot admit this, since he had defined love as a desire of something that is wanting in the lover. But Leone agrees with Holy Writ that God loves the just man, and reciprocates his devotion. True, God's love involves desire; not, however, of his own advantage, since He lacks nothing, but of his Creatures' good, that they may reach their perfection or enjoy it once reached. [18]

The second of the *Dialoghi* concerns the love which resides in creatures other than man; animals, the elements, the heavenly bodies, and the spiritual world. Its principal point, the power of love at every level of creation, recalls Pico and Ficino, but with Leone's special emphasis. "The world would not exist nor would anything be found therein, if there were no love," says Filone, "because the world and all in it can exist only in so far as it is wholly one, bound up with all it contains as an individual with his members. On the other hand, any division would involve its total destruction." [19] Love in the universe, like love in man and in God, tends toward unity.

The third dialogue takes up at great length a series of questions on the origin of love, in the course of which a number of Filone's positions are reconsidered, expanded and sometimes modified under Sofia's implacable questioning. The conversation begins with a long

---

[16] *Philosophy*, p. 35; *Dialoghi*, p. 33.
[17] *Philosophy*, p. 49; *Dialoghi*, p. 45.
[18] *Philosophy*, pp. 250-51; *Dialoghi*, pp. 214-15.
[19] *Philosophy*, pp. 190-91; *Dialoghi*, pp. 164-65.

excursus on the soul and the manner of knowing. Most significant for us is Filone's description of how the lover knows the beloved: "When the lover is wrapped in the ecstasy of contemplating that which he loves, he has no care nor thought for himself, nor does he perform any function of nature, sense, motion or reason on his own behalf, but is in everything estranged from himself belonging to and wholly transformed into the object of his love and contemplation. For the essence of the soul is its own activity; and when all its faculties are united in deep contemplation of an object, its essence is transformed into that object, which becomes its true substance. And it no longer exists as soul, and essence of him who loves, but as the actual form of the beloved." [20] Leone's unitive notion of love is thus supported by a monistic theory of knowledge. But Sofia has doubts about the disinterestedness of such a transformation. She argues that "the true nature of love is always to wish for one's own good, and not that of another." [21] For the purpose of every man's action is his own good, pleasure, and perfection; if he desires the good of another, it is on account of the pleasure he takes in that man's welfare. Surprisingly enough, Filone admits Sofia's major premise, but implies that since the beloved is a second self, and the two are really one person, such a subordination of one to the other is beside the point. The good of the beloved is truly the good of the lover; in willing the beloved's good, one indirectly wills his own. [22] It seems to me that Filone is speaking here of what the Scholastics called the *finis operis* rather than the *finis operantis;* he is dealing with the product of the lover's act and not of his conscious intention. The lover does not explicitly intend his own good in willing the good of the beloved; it is simply the inevitable result. If he means otherwise, he is contradicting his previous description of virtuous love, which under the influence of "extraordinary reason" takes no care to safeguard its own interests.

"Liebe ist ein Ring" goes the German round. At the conclusion of the third dialogue, Leone, following Pico and Ficino, describes the circle of love which is generated by God's primordial love of

[20] *Philosophy,* p. 203; *Dialoghi,* p. 176.
[21] *Philosophy,* p. 259; *Dialoghi,* p. 221.
[22] *Philosophy,* pp. 259-60; *Dialoghi,* p. 222.

creation and sweeps through the universe back to Himself. Here, as in much of his argument, he simply repeats an established position. Indeed, the *Dialoghi d'Amore* constitute a spacious repository of Renaissance ideas not only on love but on cosmology, the Bible, mythology, psychology, and medicine as well. I have singled out certain lines of thought — especially the unlimited, self-giving, and unitive nature of virtuous love, a love possible between the sexes as well as between man and God — in order to show Leone Ebreo's special place in the broad stream of Neoplatonic love philosophy, as well as to suggest something of his quality of mind — a mind that was to influence so acute a judge as John Donne.

University of North Carolina,
Chapel Hill   James A. Devereux, S. J.

To Attack Or Not To Attack: The Transformation of a Renaissance Topos

BECAUSE OF THE ADVENT of artillery, the art of warfare came under renewed close scrutiny during the Renaissance. The guidelines formulated by the strategists of antiquity had to be questioned now. The crux of the matter, when should or should not one attack and whether one should wait for the enemy or carry the fight to him, still remained; in addition, the growing obsolescence of the fortress in the light of this invention further undermined the traditional means of warfare. The question of attacking or not attacking will be analyzed here by confronting texts of Machiavelli, Guillaume Du Bellay, and Montaigne. If Machiavelli is used as the norm, as well he ought to be since he appears at the threshold of the century and casts his long shadow on all military strategists who will follow, subsequent texts, then, offer opportunities for comparison and contrast until Montaigne is reached. The author of the *Essais* transfers the subject from the realm of science and history to ethics and existential philosophy when a metaphoric meaning appears in his presentation of the subject, hence the transformation from treatise to literature.

In his typical scientific and objective manner Machiavelli delineates the pro and contra of the question; he sets up a premise and proceeds to prove both sides with ample examples for each argument. He puts up straw men so that he can better knock them down. He argues to reverse generalities in favor of specifics; therefore, he toys with the reader in order to win him over ultimately to his conclusion:

Besides the reasons adduced above, others are adduced by either side, such as that he who takes the offensive shows more spirit than he who awaits

19

an attack, and so inspires his army with more confidence; and, in addition to this, deprives the enemy of the power to utilise his own resources since he cannot avail himself of those subjects who have been despoiled...

On behalf of the other view it is said that to await the enemy's attack has many advantages; for, without any disadvantages to yourself, you can impose on him many disadvantages in the matter of provisions and of anything else of which an army has need; you can also thwart his plans owing to your having a better knowledge of the country than he has; and, again, you can oppose him with stronger forces owing to the ease with which you can bring them all together, which you could not do were they all at a distance from their homes; also, if you are routed, you can easily re-form...[1]

This discussion takes place in a chapter of the *Discourses* entitled "If it is better, when fearing attack, to begin or to await war" (II: 2). In this instance, Machiavelli wants to give the impression of ambivalence, of weighing both sides of the argument; in the final analysis, though, he weighs not in order to let matters remain in a state of suspension, of objective indecision, but rather to subsume both sides to a categorical conclusion which had already been stated at the beginning of the chapter. In other words, Machiavelli makes his way through the argumentation not for its own sake or to explore new avenues but to reinforce an a priori firm position. Of course, here, the conclusion still offers two alternatives, under two different circumstances, and therefore a somewhat relativistic stance, but each side is firmly and precisely postured to avoid any ambiguity. Open-mindedness and open-endedness are often characteristics of Humanism — not here, however; instead strong convictions and involvement dominate. Furthermore, the discourse remains on a literal level; it is rhetorical, not literary; it aims at convincing, not mystifying:

In conclusion, therefore, I say again that a ruler who has his people well armed and equipped for war, should always wait at home to wage war with a powerful and dangerous enemy and should not go out to meet him; but that one who has ill-armed subjects and a country unused to war should always meet the enemy as far away from home as he can. Both of them will in this way defend themselves better, each in his own degree. (356)

[1] *Machiavelli: The Chief Works and Others,* trans. Allan Gilbert, vol. I (Durham, N. C.: Duke University Press, 1965), pp. 354, 355.

The text by Guillaume Du Bellay opts for the defensive position; in doing so, it reflects nationalistic aims and not an anti-Machiavellian stance. Theory and abstraction are replaced by practicality, empirical evidence, dedication to the king, and the advocacy of military reforms. But before proceeding, some discussion and elaboration on this little known text is in order, a text whose authorship is still very much in question. This work, which saw four editions in the XVIth century, was first published in 1548 under the title *Instructions sur le faict de la guerre;* the second edition in 1549 stressed its sources in the title: *Instructions sur le faict de la guerre, extraictes des livres de Polybe, Frontin, Vegece, Cornazan, Machiavelle, et plusieurs autres bons autheurs.* The last edition (the last one until modern times) in 1592 offers a different title which brings out each page heading in the text: *Discipline Militaire de Messire Guillaume du Bellay, Seigneur de Langey...* This work was soon translated into the principal European languages, including English in 1589: *Instructions for the warres, amply, learnedly, and politiquely, discoursing the method of Military Discipline...* by Paule Ive. In the XVIth century, the authorship of the book was attributed to Guillaume Du Bellay and widely so accepted. But then early in the next century, through the use of internal textual evidence, François Fourquevaux attributed the work to his father Raymond de Beccarie de Pavie, sieur de Fourquevaux (1508-1574). The author of the critical edition published some twenty years ago, simply accepts this attribution but without adducing any new convincing evidence. [2] It is also quite conceivable that Rabelais may have had a hand in the composition of this work; Rabelais, who had been in the service of Du Bellay in Turin at the time the *Instructions* was composed, wrote during that period a military treatise and history, *Stratagèmes, c'est-à-dire prouesses et ruses de guerre du pieux et très célèbre chevalier de Langey, au commencement de la tierce guerre cesarienne,* of which no trace exists today. [3]

[2] Raymond de Beccarie de Pavie, sieur de Fourquevaux, *The Instructions sur le Faict de la Guerre,* ed. Gladys Dickinson (London: The Athlone Press, 1954), p. cx-cxiii.

[3] I deal with this question of authorship in a forthcoming article, "De l'authenticité des *Instructions sur le faict de la guerre*" (to be published in *Actes du Congrès Marguerite de Savoie: littérature et politique au XVIe siècle*).

The *Instructions* owe much to Machiavelli's *Art of War*; many passages amounting to many pages deal with the structure and composition of troops based on the Roman model. Both works, however, are instruments of reform; they take a strong stance against pillage, rape, and mercenary troops; instead, they advocate a national militia, that is, a draft, to insure commitment and military success. The French author, though, is more restrained in his emulation of the Romans than Machiavelli, in regard to their armaments, for example. But, of course, the chapter in the *Instructions* (Book II, ch. 3) dealing with our topos is derived essentially from Machiavelli's *Discourses*. In taking the defensive position, to wait for the enemy and not attack offensively, the French author bears in mind above all the military compaign of 1536-38 between François I and Charles V which took place in Provence. Here the king decided to fight the emperor in his own lands, even laying them to waste so that the enemy would have no food, instead of taking the battle to the emperor's ground in Italy. And this strategy did win for the king. The author of the *Instructions* makes his point on an historical occurrence and in the process happens to follow the advice given by Machiavelli, because François I fits the description of the ruler "who has his people well armed and equipped for war, should always wait at home to wage war with a powerful and dangerous enemy and should not go out to meet him." Therefore, the French strategist is quite categorical:

Wherefore I do make no doubt to rest upon this conclusion, that is that every Prince ought to have a regarde, before hee enter into the countrie of another Prince his neighbor that is as mightie as himselfe, and moreover, as wee see the King is. And besides the reasons aforesayd, he that is assayled may attend the comming of his enemies into his countrie with a great advantage: for that he may famish them, and take from them the use of all things appertayning unto a Campe, without the danger of having any lacke of victuall on his side ... All these things considered, I may conclude that he is in greater hazard that doth assayle his neighbor, than he that doth stay for to resist him: as the comming of the above sayd Emperour doth give me occasion to speake, which is the fittest example that I may alleadge for this matter. [4]

[4] *Instructions for the warres. Amply, learnedly, and politiquely, discoursing the method of militarie discipline. Originally written in French by William de [sic] Bellay of Langey.* Translated by Paule Ive ... at London (Printed for Thomas Man and Tobie Coode, 1589), pp. 141, 142.

The author of the *Instructions* proves Machiavelli's point: when facing a strong enemy it is wise to battle him on one's own grounds, but he does not offer alternatives or other examples from history, as in the *Discourses,* that may also substantiate other avenues. The humanist, then, yields to the propagandist; open-mindedness and the weighing process yield to a narrowness of viewpoint; intellectualism succumbs to nationalism. Machiavelli at least goes through the motions of thesis, antithesis and synthesis whereas the author of the *Instructions* emphasizes the success of François I's campaign in Provence. The immediate empirical wins over the past and the theoretical. The French military tactician has used the Italian theoretician to his advantage; he has simply taken what he needs which happens to coincide with his counterpart's conclusion, but the critical element is lacking; the treatise replaces the dialogue; the one-sided historian disregards the more typical plurivalent humanistic historian who seeks the image of man behind events.

Montaigne assimilates both Machiavelli and the *Instructions* and integrates them in a scheme of arguments producing ambivalence and reducing man's intelligence to the whim of fortune; the literal military framework found in his predecessors has been transformed into a metaphoric situation pitting man against himself, against others, against the cosmos. Whereas Machiavelli and the author of the *Instructions* eventually take a stance and leave man's choice up to his will or to an established framework, Montaigne presents both sides of the question, with ample examples and argumentation in each case, finds all events equally valid in the circumstances they occurred and therefore does not choose one over the other. It is true that his suspension of judgment may be caused by the subject and the title of the essay in which the discussion takes place "Of the uncertainty of our judgment" (I: 47), but this questioning of facts and knowledge earmarks indeed all of Montaigne's thinking.

In presenting his argumentation, Montaigne draws principally and in heavy amounts (one page of essay text in each case) from two domains: Plutarch and the *Instructions;* the echoes from Machiavelli's *Discourses* only comprise a few lines and may have been elicited via the *Instructions.* In citing the battle of Pharsala between Caesar and Pompey, an episode taken from Plutarch, Montaigne views hypothetically the other side of the coin; Pompey had lost because he had waited for Caesar at a standstill.

> But if Caesar had lost, might not the contrary have been said just as well: that the strongest and stiffest posture is that which a man stands planted without budging, and that whoever has stopped in his march, holding in and saving up his strength within himself for the time of need, has a great advantage over one who is in motion and has already wasted half his breath in running? Besides, an army, being a body made up of so many different parts, cannot possibly move with such precision in this fury as not to alter or break up its battle array, or in such a way that the swiftest will not be at grips before his companion comes to support him. [5]

The didacticism of Montaigne's predecessors is absent here; instead he depicts man in a fortuitous and accidental framework. The need to show the reverse side of the coin will bring about a lucidity toward the cause-effect relationship of events and its arbitrariness.

The episode of the campaign between François and Charles V in Provence derived from the *Instructions* gives a clear indication of how Montaigne purposely distorts a text to suit his viewpoint. In a sentence over one page long he places himself in the frame of mind of the king, who first weighs the advantages and then the disadvantages of invading Italy or of waiting for the emperor in France, but he never actually states that the king made a decision or whether it was the right one; he is much more interested in constructing an argumentative edifice than a forthright rhetorical situation. This prolix sentence, punctuated by very frequent semicolons which do not necessarily separate independent clauses, may reproduce the travails of the king's mind and decision making process; however, by its very abusive length it may also point to Montaigne's manipulation and orchestration of the subject, to a delight in toying with it and mystifying the reader. Montaigne thus alters the meaning of the text from the *Instructions* since he does not follow its nationalistic and propagandistic conclusion, but instead he stresses the king's indecision: "And there was no lack of examples on both sides" (209). The fact that the king actually chose to wait for the enemy is almost overlooked and is merely mentioned before Mon-

---

[5] *The Complete Essays of Montaigne,* trans. Donald M. Frame (Stanford Univ. Press, 1965), pp. 207-08.

taigne starts presenting the case of the king who may have to await Charles V, but the reasons for taking the fight to the enemy certainly do not outweigh the one for awaiting him: "Nonetheless, he chose to recall the forces he had beyond the mountains and to watch the enemy come to him... For he may have imagined on the other hand that being at home and among friends, he could not fail to have plenty of all commodities..." (208).

The specific argumentation taken from Machiavelli's *Discourses* also offers the pro and con of the question without favoring one over the other. Since these examples occur at the end of the essay, just as the same ones had also come at the end of the chapter in the *Instructions*, it is not too bold to conjecture that their presence in Montaigne echoes the *Instructions*, but such a presence does not preclude a direct knowledge of the *Discourses* as well. In this instance, Montaigne distills the subject matter to a simple few lines: "Scipio thought it much better to go and attack his enemy's territory in Africa than to defend his own and fight in Italy where he was; and this worked out well for him. On the other hand, Hannibal, in that same war ruined himself by abandoning the conquest of a foreign country to go and defend his own. The Athenians, having left the enemy in their territory to go over into Sicily, had Fortune against them; but Agathocles, king of Syracuse, found her favorable when he crossed over into Africa and left the war at home" (209). Montaigne is intent on a non-committed stance; he depicts a situation and then lets the reader make up his own mind or remain as suspended as he himself is.

Yet in this particular case Montaigne takes away the initiative from man; whereas Machiavelli prefers to assert his will in any situation, and, in the context of the subject before us, he very clearly delineates the options according to circumstances. And although the *Instructions* rhetorically raise both sides of the question, only the king's actions are the right ones. Montaigne, however, suggests a certain submission, a helplessness before events. The Machiavellian self-assertive drive and strong viewpoint have yielded to an even-handedness, an acceptance couched in a semblance of serenity; the limitlessness of man has now evolved to a realization of his limitation; the decisiveness of man, as seen in the *Instructions*, has now been transformed into the fallibility of reason and speech. Therefore, Montaigne does not always reproduce his readings but he interprets them, or rather misinterprets them to his needs; without meaning to, the humanist here joins hands with the scholastic who had distorted classical texts. Montaigne's conclusion is unequivocal but either specifically disparate from his reference or in function of his own sentiments which here parallel more Machiavelli's obsession with fortune than the *Discourses'* often rhetorical purposes:

> Thus we are quite wont to say, with reason, that events and outcomes depend for the most part, especially in war, on Fortune, who will not fall into line and subject herself to our discourse and foresight... But if you take it rightly, it seems that our counsels and deliberations depend just as much on Fortune, and that she involves our discourse also in her confusion and uncertainty. "We reason rashly and inconsiderately," says Timaeus in Plato, "because, like ourselves, our discourse has in it a large element of chance." (209)

A comparative study of three Renaissance texts dealing with the notion of to attack or not to attack raises two interrelated questions: what concept of humanism is derived from it, if any? and what delineates rhetoric from literature? Even from the one chapter of the *Discourses* used here, the Machiavellian universe already becomes quite apparent; a somewhat firm will and rather categorical opinions set, however, in a relativistic framework; the argumentation of both sides of an issue does not aim so much at weighing a subject matter as at formulating a conclusion where man remains as much as possible master of the situation. The chapter from the *Instructions* follows in the same vein; decisions remain within man's grasp and are slightly simplified because the rational weighing process is subverted. This view of man may explain the underlying irony present in Montaigne's use of the *Instructions* episode. When Montaigne poses the situation, all initiative has been taken away from man; a clear curve is drawn from self-assertion to submission, to making the best of the inevitable, of the goddess Fortune. In the *Essais* the measure of man has been realigned and placed in a more human perspective; the self now assimilates to existing conditions. The analysis of these three texts also reveals a shift from rhetoric to literature, that is, from conviction to ambiguity, from the literal to a multidimensional figurative plane. The realm of warfare has been transfigured into the awesome human situation. Montaigne imparts to the topos under discussion reverberations of the human destiny; are we masters of it or not. When the clearness of rhetoric yields to the grey zone of the thinking process, when symmetry or asymmetry becomes organic structure, when the fact is suddenly metaphor, then literature appears.

Duke University   Marcel Tetel

The Fascination of *Il Principe*

T HERE IS NO SHORTAGE of interpretations of both Machiavelli and *Il Principe*. There is *Il Principe* as a satire, as a warning to tyrants, as an attack upon the Church, as a mirror for princes, as a fantasy, as a conception of the state as a work of art. And Machiavelli is variously seen as an anguished humanist, an objective scientist, a fervent Italian patriot, a desperate office-seeker, a tool of the Devil, a revolutionary innovator. [1]

The purpose of this paper is not to present a new interpretation of Machiavelli or of his treatise. Rather I want to suggest one reason for the existence of so many conflicting interpretations. For, as Sir Isaiah Berlin writes, "There is something surprising about the sheer number of interpretations of Machiavelli's political opinions." [2] And I would further suggest that the reason why we still respond with fascinated interest to *Il Principe* is not because it is relevant to our times or even consistent with itself but because it is capable of being seen in so many conflicting ways. Like Keats' urn, Machiavelli's treatise teases us out of thought by offering us a vision which is not historical, certainly not philosophical, but fundamentally poetic.

It is, of course, no great discovery to realize that Machiavelli is an artist. But it is a rather different thing to realize that the power of *Il Principe* is the power of art. What Machiavelli gives us is not pure art, but the ability of *Il Principe* to draw our interest today depends upon its drama, its ambiguity, its paradox and irony, its heightening and suppressing. One cannot, in a short paper, comment on all aspects of Machiavelli's art. I shall treat the two which seem to me of prime importance: the ambiguity of the Prince's purpose

---

[1] For a survey of various interpretations of *Il Principe*, see Isaiah Berlin, "The Originality of Machiavelli," in *Studies on Machiavelli*, ed. Myron Gilmore, Sansoni, 1972, Florence, pp. 149-206.

[2] Isaiah Berlin, p. 149.

and the dramatic nature of Machiavelli's vision of the world in which the Prince struggles to fulfill his purpose.

Certainly there is no ambiguity concerning Machiavelli's purpose in presenting *Il Principe* to Lorenzo de' Medici: he wanted to draw attention to his own special qualifications for a position in Lorenzo's government. But the Prince's purpose is never defined. Unlimited by human sympathies or weaknesses, neither good nor evil, an instrument neither of God nor of destiny, the Prince has apparently only one purpose — survival. There are real, historical princes in Machiavelli's treatise, many of them. But the Prince is not like them, nor is he like any human being who has ever lived. He seems to have put off mortality. He neither eats nor sleeps. He does not fall in love and he is careful to keep his hands off his subjects' wives and daughters. He has no recreations, no pleasure of any kind. When it is necessary to be cruel he can be cruel, but he never develops an appetite for cruelty as real men have been known to do. He is unconcerned with ceremonies and gorgeous trappings. Secret and self-contained, he has no friends, no favorites, no confidants, no one to share his burdens. As far as that goes, he has no burdens. The cares that weigh so heavily on Shakespeare's kings do not touch him. He has no great designs, no noble plans. While it may be useful for him to do some great deed to give proof of his prowess, he has no obligation to behave aggressively since his object is apparently simply to maintain his status (*mantenere lo stato*) and preserve what we would call his image.

He certainly does not exist to serve his people. They are a craven lot, not to be trusted. He is not obliged to consider their happiness or their prosperity except insofar as these matters affect his security. "At convenient seasons of the year" he will provide festivals and shows; he will recognize merit and encourage peaceful industry; occasionally he will even mingle with the citizens. But his overriding concern is with *lo stato,* and whatever *lo stato* is, it is emphatically not the citizens.

It is *lo stato* which lies at the heart of the ambiguity of *Il Principe.* J. H. Hexter's careful analysis [3] indicates that for Machiavelli

[3] *"Il Principe* and *lo stato," Studies in the Renaissance* (1957), pp. 113-138.

lo stato is not a body politic; "it is an instrument of exploitation, the mechanism the prince uses to get what he wants" (p. 134). "The effectual truth, the truth that counts, the only truth that matters to Machiavelli in *Il Principe,* the only truth that matters to the prince himself, is whether the prince wins out, keeps what he has, holds *lo stato,* or loses out, loses what he had, loses *lo stato*" (p. 125). I think this is a fair statement. The Prince's only aim is to gain, to hold, to maintain, not to lose *lo stato. Lo stato* is not a state, a territory, a populace. It is rather the Prince's status; it naturally requires territory and citizens, but it is the Prince's own possession.

As Joseph Mazzeo remarks, Machiavelli's universe "is open at the farther end."[4] That is, the immediate surroundings are fairly well defined, but when one looks toward the distant goal there is nothing to see. The Prince has no future; everything is now. His goal is his status; his success is to have, to maintain, not to lose. He does not build anything. Nothing develops during his reign. It is precisely this quality of timelessness that Montaigne marked as a flaw in Machiavelli's treatise. Is the Prince allowed to break his word whenever it is convenient? Very well, says Montaigne. It may work once. "But that is not how things happen. He is always making similar bargains; he concludes more than one peace, and more than one treaty, in his life. It is gain that tempts him to his first breach of faith ... but this initial gain is followed by endless losses, and the prince is debarred by this instance of faithlessness from all chance of amity and negotiation."[5]

Sir Isaiah Berlin, in an essay which depends heavily on the *Discorsi,* supposes that Machiavelli has an ultimate goal other than the Prince's survival. The goal is "that which for a Renaissance reader Pericles had seen embodied in his ideal Athens, Livy had found in the old Roman Republic, that of which Tacitus and Juvenal lamented the decay and death in their own time. These seem to Machiavelli the best hours of mankind and, Renaissance humanist that he is, he wishes to restore them."[6] I think this is quite true of the *Discorsi,*

[4] "The Poetry of Power: Machiavelli's Literary Vision," *Review of National Literatures* (1970), p. 59.
[5] From the essay "On Presumption," trans. J. M. Cohen, Penguin Classics, p. 209.
[6] "The Originality of Machiavelli," p. 169.

31

but nothing in *Il Principe* even suggests that such values are important to a ruler. No doubt Sir Isaiah is correct when he writes that for Machiavelli there is a "moral ideal for which he thinks no sacrifice too great—the welfare of the *patria*..." [7] But the Prince has no *patria*. He simply has a *stato*—a status—to maintain. There is no end beyond that. Consequently Cesare Borgia appears in *Il Principe* as an example to be imitated. There is not the slightest hint that Cesare had a great vision of the *patria*, of an ordered and harmonious society based on civic virtues of courage, fortitude and magnanimity. For Cesare, conquest was an end in itself. What he would have done with his *stato*, had he been able to maintain it, is not even suggested. He lost his *stato* because, at a critical moment, he yielded to a human weakness and fell ill.

Machiavelli's treatise shows us a prince who is not a human being. This imagined ruler strives to achieve and maintain a *stato* which has no purpose except to exist. One reason why there are so many conflicting interpretations of *Il Principe* it that we all feel a need to fill this vacuum, to supply a purpose for the Prince. We are disturbed by a vision of politics and statecraft which suggests that there is some value more important than accepted standards of moral and ethical behavior but never says what this value is. Surely there must be an interpretation which will rationalize this vision. So we proceed to supply one. But, if I read *Il Principe* correctly, Machiavelli is unconcerned with purposes. *Il Principe* is a work that deals with means, not ends. Whether it is the result of conscious art or not, Machiavelli's ambiguity regarding the Prince's purpose produces effects not uncommon to works of conscious art: the sense of mystery, of a dimension beyond reason and logic, of a refusal to spell out what must be caught by the sympathetic imagination.

The other aspect of Machiavelli's art—the dramatic nature of his vision of the Prince's world—is fitfully but powerfully displayed. This is not a sustained vision; we catch glimpses of it, frequently in the midst of a detailed treatment of a fairly dull topic. It is in the chapter on mixed monarchies, for instance, that Machiavelli remarks that "the desire to acquire possessions is a very natural and ordinary

[7] "The Originality of Machiavelli," p. 182.

thing...." [8] Earlier in the same chapter he has told us that "men must be either caressed or else annihilated...." (p. 9). Involved in these statements are two primary assumptions that influence the entire work, i.e. that aggresion and greed are perfectly natural and blameless when they succeed, and that halfway measures are ruinous. Yet Machiavelli does not distinguish these statements as axioms nor does he argue their validity. The reader will find it difficult to remember or to care about the failures of Louis XII, discussed in so much detail in this chapter. But the two passages just quoted are unforgettable, for they help to define Machiavelli's vision of the world in which the Prince must survive.

It is this vision that draws us to *Il Principe,* not any hope to find the truth about politics. The notion that Machiavelli is a realist dies hard, but it was obvious to Montaigne nearly 400 years ago that Machiavelli was merely arguing a case: "Machiavelli's arguments, for example, were substantial enough for their subject, yet they were quite easy to contest... for our arguments have little foundation except that of experience, and the variety of human events furnishes us with infinite examples of every possible kind." [9] What holds *Il Principe* together and draws us to it is not its rational argument but its vision of unremitting conflict, or an ironic universe which punishes good and rewards evil, of the capricious goddess Fortuna who yields her favors to the reckless young, of men who are only half free striving to stem the tide of disaster.

Machiavelli's Prince lives on the razor's edge. There are only two possibilities: success or ruin. Nowhere does Machiavelli say this, but his style makes it clear that politics is a matter of life and death. The lion may be trapped, the fox destroyed by wolves. The injury the Prince does to a man must be such that the Prince need not fear his vengeance. Incompetent mercenary captains will ruin the Prince, competent ones will oppress him. The account of Cesare Borgia clearly suggests that Cesare failed to consolidate his conquests because of a mortal illness. We may be surprised to discover that

[8] *The Prince and the Discourses,* introduction by Max Lerner, translator not named, Modern Library, 1940, p. 13. Subsequent quotations are from this edition.
[9] "On Presumption," Penguin ed., pp. 216-217.

Cesare recovered, fled to Naples, was held a prisoner, sent to Spain, escaped from prison and finally died in a minor skirmish. This undramatic demise does not appear in *Il Principe,* though it had taken place at least five years before Machiavelli wrote his treatise. The death of Ramiro de Lorqua, violent and dramatic, is the sort of end that fascinates Machiavelli.

Machiavelli's world is a place of treachery and betrayal. This premise he enunciates clearly, though rather late in his treatise: "men will always be false to you unless they are compelled by necessity to be true" (p. 89). So the Prince must beware of flatterers and of secretaries who think of their own interests. There are no rules for choosing wise counsellors, only cautions for avoiding treacherous ones. The people, of course, will desert the Prince when he most needs them. As for other princes, it is hardly necessary to point out that they can never be trusted. Nor are there any safe policies; "all are doubtful" (p. 84).

What then is the Prince's reward if he survives in this treacherous world? At best, glory, no small reward to Machiavelli's mind. But glory is not a persistent theme in *Il Principe.* More frequently it appears that the Prince's reward for surviving is survival—to have *lo stato,* to maintain *lo stato,* not to lose *lo stato.* It is not clear that his people can expect anything beyond not being taxed. One might argue that the people are rewarded by domestic order, that efficient government will preserve their lives and states. In fact, Machiavelli does not say just this, though he hints at it. The treatise is so narrowly focussed on the Prince that we can only guess at what Machiavelli thinks about the benefits that may incidentally befall the citizens.

Anyone who is familiar with *Il Principe* will surely point out that the famous final chapter is at odds with much of what I have said. Indeed it is, and it is also at odds with much of what Machiavelli himself said in the preceding chapters. The final chapter does give the Prince a clearly defined purpose: the liberation of Italy from "this barbarous domination" (p. 98). Italy is the *patria;* its freedom and national pride are the values which supersede ordinary morality. In the name of Italian freedom the Prince may do anything. So, at least, we may surmise. The fact is that the final chapter is so disconnected

34

from all the rest of *Il Principe* and so tied to a particular time and place that it is difficult to see it as a necessary part of the whole treatise. Are those obedient people shedding tears of gratitude and opening their doors to the liberator the same bunch who abandoned the Prince whenever he had need of them? Will such people be ready to follow any standard if only there is someone to raise it? No doubt this final chapter is as dramatic as anything else in *Il Principe*, but the style, with its passionate enthusiasm, its rhetorical flourishes, tells us that we have moved into another world. It is not the timeless world of *lo stato*, the Prince's own possession to be acquired, maintained, held. It is the historical world, a part of which is Italy. Italy is *la patria*, and she is not to be acquired or maintained or held; she is to be *redeemed*. The attitude of religious fervor which Machiavelli shows in this chapter is strongly at odds with the cold detachment of all that precedes it.

So *Il Principe* continues to fascinate us precisely because Machiavelli has left so much that is undefined. For all its references to history, *Il Principe* is a profoundly unhistorical work. It presents a vision of a permanent, timeless state of conflict, a struggle which leads to nothing beyond mere survival in a world where all decisions are matters of life and death and the state *is* the Prince. Nowhere in his treatise does Machiavelli openly proclaim these points. Instead, like Keats' "cold pastoral," Machiavelli's cold courtesy book opens up a vision to which we respond with puzzled fascination.

University of Tennessee-Knoxville   THOMAS WHEELER

The Ant, the Field-Mouse, and the Mole: Webster's *The White Devil*, V. iv. 100

A S CORNELIA, MARCELLO'S MOTHER, is preparing his corpse for burial, she speaks to the attendant ladies and to her other son, Flamineo the fratricide:

> I'll give you a saying which my grandmother
> Was wont, when she heard the bell toll, to sing o'er
> Unto her lute. [1]

> (V. iv. 92-94)

And then follows one of the most touching elegies in all of drama:

> Call for the robin-red-breast and the wren
> Since o'er shady groves they hover,
> And with leaves and flow'rs do cover
> The friendless bodies of unburied men.
> Call unto his funeral dole
> The ant, the field-mouse, and the mole
> To rear him hillocks, that shall keep him warm,
> And (when gay tombs are robb'd) sustain no harm, —
> But keep the wolf far thence, that's foe to men,
> For with his nails he'll dig them up agen.

The animal symbolism has been explained in part by Webster's editors, [2] for we have sufficient commentary on the robin, the wren, and the wolf. An old folk-belief has it that the robin was said to cover

---

[1] The quotations are from J. R. Brown's edition of *The White Devil* (London, 1960) in the Revels Plays.

[2] See not only Brown's notes on the passage (p. 165) but those in Lucas's edition as well (London, 1958), p. 205.

the face of a dead body with moss, sometimes covering indeed the whole body. Drayton in *The Owl* (1604) wrote,

> Covering with moss the dead, unclosèd eye
> The little redbreast teacheth charity.

The wren was believed to be the robin's wife: "The robin redbreast and the wren / Are God Almighty's cock and hen." And the wolf dug up the bodies of those who had been murdered, eating all parts of the body except the face. Webster himself alludes to the superstition of the wolf seeking out the murdered in *The Duchess of Malfi*:

> The wolf shall find her grave, and scrape it up:
> Not to devour the corpse, but to discover
> The horrid murder.
>
> (IV. ii. 309-311)

But editors seem to be silent on the ant, the field-mouse, and the mole—perhaps because their common occupation of underground builders, surely appropriate for tomb-makers, is so evident. But there are other qualities that they have in animal lore that may explain their appearance in Cornelia's dirge.

The field-mouse and the mole share, according to Topsell,[3] a compassion for their fellows: if a field-mouse falls into a vessel of water from which he cannot escape, "they help one another, by letting down their tails":

and if their tails be too short, then they lengthen them by this means: they take one anothers tail in their mouth, and so hang two or three in length, until the Mouse which was fallen down take hold on the neathermost, which being performed, they all of them draw her out.

The same kind of compassion is seen in the mole. There is a story by Gillius reported by Topsell[4] that shows this quality:

When I had (saith he) put down into the earth as earthen pot made of purpose with a narrow mouth to take Moles, it fortuned that within short

---

[3] Edward Topsell, *The History of Four-Footed Beasts and Serpents and Insects* (London, 1658), I. 395. Topsell's *History* is largely based on Conrad Gesner's *Historiae Animalium*, 1551.

[4] Topsell, I, 390.

space as a blind Mole came along she fell into it and could not get forth again, but lay there whinning; one of her fellowes which followed her seeing [sic] his mate taken, heaved up the earth above the pot, and with her nose cast in so much, till she had raised up her companion to the brim and was ready to come forth: by which in that blind creature confined to darkness, doth not only appear a wonderful work of Almighty God, that endoweth them with skill to defend, and wisely to provide for their own safety, but also planted in them such a natural and mutual love one to another, which is so much the more admirable....

The ant, of course, has always been so renowned for industry that sluggards are advised by the writer of the Book of Proverbs to "consider her ways and be wise." Christopher Smart, in his "On the Omniscience of God," describes the "sage, industrious Ant," as "the wisest insect, / The best economist of the field"; Milton saw the "parsimonious Emmet" as a "Pattern of just equality perhaps / Hereafter, join'd in her popular tribes / Of commonalty," [5] following an old belief that "nature hath given them for their degree and order, a constant and absolute perfection." [6] Bacon may have scorned them, as he did "men of experiment" who "only collect and use" (Novum Organum, Book I, Aphorism XCV); but usually they were commended for their prudence, nibbling off parts of their collected grain so that it would not germinate, dividing larger seeds from the smaller, and drying the seeds that were wet. [7]

Thomas Mouffet in his *Theatre of Insects* waxes close to the ecstatic in describing their "house":

Histories do mightily magnifie the Pyramids, and trenches of *Egypt,* and the Labyrinth of *Crete.* But no man can sufficiently set forth the excellent work of trenches that the Ants make, the figure, the magnificence, the turnings, windings, and revolutions thereof: for these by an unspeakable prudence, beyond all mans art, make houses under ground with such strange turnings, that they open only the way that is unaccesible to others, and is not possible for any that would do them wrong to enter at.... This divine little creature fetcheth the fashion of its building from heaven, either because their multitudes need room, or their excellence required the best.

[5] *Paradise Lost,* VII. 485-489.
[6] Mouffet (or Muffet) published his *Insectorum sive Minimorum Animalium Theatrum* in 1634. Translated, it became Volume III in Topsell's history. This praise by Mouffet is at III, 1074.
[7] Beryl Rowland, *Animals with Human Faces* (Knoxville, Tenn., 1973), page 4.

And then, in a strange and unexpected parallel with Webster's elevation of the "hillocks" over "gay tombs," we have this in Mouffet:

And this is the manner of their building, plain indeed, and within the ground, as were the houses of the wise men of elder times, before that pride, and the head-strong ambition of *Ninus* invented to build up towers to heaven. Since his death, shall I speak of Kings or Princes? Truly there are some Citizens of the lower bench, who with extraordinary charge do build up, not an Ant-hill, but *Mausoleum,* or a prison for their bodyes, and adorn it with all the cost and art they can; worthy they are indeed to be devoured by Pismires whilest they live, that dying by the force of a wise Creature, they may suffer for their folly. *(ibid.)*

But their great skill in building, not even their prudence and equitable distribution, exhaust their virtue: their modesty, as Mouffet calls it, cannot be passed over.

For though they go in a narrow way, yet there are no brawlings, contentions, or strivings for it, not yet any murmurings, or fightings, or slaughters amongst they for place (as it is usual amongst proud men.) ... [E]ach of them is ready modestly rather to passe by an injury, then Waspishly to offer one. (III, 1076)

To all of this, he adds another quality which makes the ant a proper custodian of Marcello's corpse: they prove their "cleanliness" by attending to their own dead: "they carry out their dead in the husks or bladders of trees and Corn, as of old time the *Romans* buried their dead in pots" *(ibid.).*

The great French naturalist deRéaumur enlarges upon this honoring of the dead accepted by the ancients:

Not only Pliny but all the ancient naturalists laud the ant because they honor their dead in the same manner that we honor our own. They assure us that each formicary has its cemetary. It is believed, furthermore, that the dead ant is not carried thither till after it has been placed in a coffin: but that the living do not have to trouble to make one, because empty husks or follicles of certain seeds furnish coffins all but ready-made.... [9]

He cannot help adding that "what the erudite of former times seriously proclaimed to other savants would to-day scarcely be recounted by credulous nurses to their nurselings."

[8] Mouffet, III, 1075.
[9] *The Natural History of Ants,* translated and annotated by William M. Wheeler (New York, 1926), pp. 132-133.

40

But in an earlier, less scientific age, Mouffet had described the ant as a paragon of virtues:

Since therefore (to wind up all in a few words) they are so exemplary for their great piety, prudence, justice, valour, temperance, modesty, charity, friendship, frugality, perseverance, industry, and art; it is no wonder that Plato in *Phedone,* hath determined, that they who without the help of Philosophy have led a civil life by custom or from their own diligence, they had their souls from Ants, and when they die they are turned to Ants again. (III, 1078)

The ant, the field-mouse, and the mole are summoned in Cornelia's dirge not just because they are excellent builders. They all three share in a compassion that is absent in nearly all the characters in Webster's drama; the ant is particularly solicitous about burying its dead, and its house excited the admiration of the ancient naturalists. Surely if the ant is to rear Marcello hillocks to keep him warm, the pattern of its building, as Mouffet assures us, has been fetched from heaven.

University of Virginia   I. B. CAUTHEN, JR.

Bentley Redivivus:
Some Emendations in *Paradise Lost*

D R. BENTLEY HAS JUSTLY been ridiculed for some of his
emendations of *Paradise Lost*. Yet now and then he deserves
praise. For example, he found that the text, on the Sixth Day of
Creation, read

> Let th' Earth bring forth Fowle living in her kinde.
>
> (7.451)

He observed that this is the Authorized Version's

Let the earth bring forth the living creature after his kind. (Gen. 1.24)

and that the fowls were created on the preceding day. As Mr. Hughes
says, Bentley's emendation of *fowle* to *soul* is "inevitable." But alas!
too often Bentley shows that it is dangerous to meddle with a text,
manuscript or printed. All emendation is suspect, often showing the
ignorance of the emender. So while writing this paper I have often
asked myself: "Are you being as foolish as Bentley was?" Nevertheless, there must be emendation. Following the table of errata
in the first edition of *Paradise Lost* is the exhortation: "Other literal
faults the Reader of himself may correct."

Let us consider the passage telling how the Children of Israel, in
the Wilderness, desired Moses as a mediator between themselves and
Jehovah. In the first edition, it runs:

> The voice of God
> To mortal ear is dreadful; they beseech
> That Moses might report to them his will,
> And terror cease; he grants them their desire.
>
> (12.235-8)

43

This is revised in the second edition, to read:

> They beseech
> That Moses might report to them his will,
> And terror cease; he grants what they besaught.

That is, *what they besaught* is substituted for *them their desire*. The change is made to carry forward the word *beseech* ending the second line above. But *besaught* is the only past tense in a passage of a hundred and fifty lines using either the vivid present tense or the future tense. Indeed, all the narrative in the Twelfth Book is thus vividly written. Why this awkward exception? The past tense is not even correct, for Moses is yet to come. So I emend to *beseech*, obtaining

> They *beseech*
> That Moses might report to them his will
> And terror cease; he grants what they *beseech*.

As I shall show, such identical endings of lines not far apart are frequent in Milton.

Let us now look at a passage in Adam's view of the horrors of warfare:

> A band select from forage drives
> A herd of beeves ...
>   or fleecy Flock,
> Ewes and thir bleating Lambs over the plaine,
> Thir bootie; scarce with Life the Shepherds flye,
> But call in aide, which tacks a bloody Fray.

(11.646-51)

The word *tacks* (t-a-c-k-s) is in the second edition emended to *makes,* giving *makes a bloody Fray.* The weak word *makes* is thus substituted for *tacks,* unintelligible to editors. It is not a poet's revision. Who did it? In asking the question, I put myself in Bentley's shoes, for he imagined an acquaintance of Milton's whom he calls a "hardy editor," a "persona of an editor," an "interpolater," as responsible for what Bentley stigmatizes the forgeries in the poem, that is, the passages which to him were "silly," "impertinent," "spurious," "trash." The device of blaming an editor did not perish with Bentley, though the villain is now called a collaborator. Such a person has been assigned to Marlowe by those who dislike the comic scenes in *Faustus;* so that one of my friends has written: "It is generally believed that Marlowe's soaring pen was incapable of the comic scenes and that a collaborator furnished them." To me, those comic scenes are authentic Marlowe. To return to Milton's *tacks a bloody Fray,* it seems to me an Anglicizing of the Italian *attaccare la battaglia,* frequent in *Orlando Furioso,* which means *begin the battle.* So Milton says that the shepherds get protectors who engage in bloody conflict with the foragers. The change to *makes* cannot be his.

The work of Bentley's "hardy editor" I find also in the Almighty Father's initial speech in the heavenly council in Book Three. Since my most important emendations are there, and are justified, if at all, only by the entire passage, I read the speech as emended:

> Onely begotten Son, seest thou what rage
> Transports our adversarie, whom no bounds
> Prescrib'd, no barrs of Hell, nor all the chains
> Heapt on him there, nor yet the main Abyss
> Wide interrupt can hold; so bent he seems
> On desperate reveng, that shall redound
> Upon his own rebellious head. And now
> Through all restraint broke loose he wings his way
> Not far off Heav'n, in the precincts of light,
> Directly towards the new created World,
> And Man there plac't, with purpose to assay
> If him by force he can destroy, or worse,
> By some false guile pervert; and shall pervert,
> For man will heark'n to his glozing lyes,
> And easily transgress the sole Command,
> Sole pledge of his obedience: So will *fall,*
> Hee and his faithless Progenie: whose fault?
> Whose but his own? ingrate, he had of mee
> All he could have; I made him just and right,
> Sufficient to have stood, though free to *fall.*
> Such I created all th' Ethereal Powers
> And Spirits, both them who stood and them who *fell.*
> Freely they stood who stood, and *fell* who *fell.*
> Not free, what proof could they have givn sincere
> Of true allegiance, constant Faith or Love,
> Where onely what they needs must do, appeard,
> Not what they would? what praise could they receive?

45

> When Will and Reason (Reason also is choice)
> Useless and vain, of freedom both despoild,
> Made passive both, had servd necessitie,
> Not mee. They therefore as to right belongd,
> So were created, nor can justly accuse
> Thir maker, or thir making. or thir Fate,
> As if predestination over-rul'd
> Thir will, disposed by absolute Decree
> Or high foreknowledge; they themselves decreed
> Thir own revolt, not I; if I foreknew,
> Foreknowledge had no influence on their *fall*,
> Which had no less prov'd certain unforeknown.
> So without least impulse or shadow of Fate,
> Or aught by me immutablie foreseen,
> They trespass, Authors to themelves in all
> Both what they judge and what they choose; for so
> I formd them free, and free they must remain,
> Till they enthrall themselves: I else must change
> Thir nature, and revoke the high Decree
> Unchangeable, Eternal, which ordain'd
> Thir freedom, they themselves ordain'd thir *fall*.
> The first sort by thir own suggestion *fell*,
> Self-tempted, self-deprav'd: Man *falls* deceiv'd
> By the other first: Man therefore shall find grace,
> The other none: in Mercy and Justice both,
> Through Heav'n and Earth, so shall my glorie excel,
> But Mercy first and last shall brightest shine.

(3.80-134)

The subject, reiterated, is the Fall of Man. The speech puts rationally what the whole poem gives in action. The Almighty Father develops in logic the subject announced in the first lines of the epic:

> Of Mans First Disobedience, and the Fruit
> Of that Forbidden Tree, whose mortal taste
> Brought Death into the World, and all our woe,
> With loss of Eden, till one greater Man
> Restore us, and regain the blisful Seat.

(1.1-5)

"Man's first disobedience" is the Fall, essential in seventeenth-century theology. That Fall implies the work of the "Greater Man," who is to *re*store and *re*gain what man lost by disobedience. Without the Fall, there is no place for a *Re*deemer. But though the Almighty's speech is essential to the theological idea of Milton's epic, its impor-

46

tance in the plot is even more immediate. The Father, looking down from Heaven, sees Satan flying toward the world to attack man. Thus far, Satan, escaping from Hell, has seemed to prosper in his attempt to thwart the Almighty's purpose. Is he to succeed in ruining man? But the Almighty, watching him as he approaches the world, speaks. The scene is dramatic in its exact timing. God's speech sets the limits of Satan's accomplishment before the Adversary has begun to act. Though the Devil does cause man's Fall, that Fall is not a Satanic triumph. On the contrary, it reveals the divine providence that uses Satan as one of its instruments. The reader is assured that in tempting man to fall—the chief concern of Milton's plot—Satan's activity is futile, his success illusory. So Milton here shows that ability to integrate plot and idea in which he surpasses all other epic poets.

The Almighty's speech shows also how for Milton rhetorical effect and idea go hand in hand. The word *fall* is iterated not merely for emphasis of thought, but for metrical effect. In the fifty-five lines I read, you heard *fall,* in various forms, nine times; six times it came in an emphatic position — for Milton, who handles verses as entities — at the end of a line; two of the repetitions are paired in that position, giving identical rimes. But Milton's metrical skill appears in full vigor only after my emendations. In the usual texts, his intention is twice negated. One of these perversions was noted by Bentley, with a perception that atones for some of his absurdities. In the early editions, he read:

> Such I created all th' Ethereal Powers
> And Spirits; both Them who stood and Them who faild;
> Freely they stood who stood, and *fell* who *fell.*

> (3.100-3)

Bentley comments: "Both the Antitheton and the Repetition in the next line show that the Author gave it:

> Both Them who stood, and Them who *fell:*
> Freely they stood who stood and *fell* who *fell.*"

This emendation is also "inevitable," though I never have seen it remarked on. But having begun so well, Bentley did not continue. After a few lines, the texts offer a similar perversion:

47

> If I foreknew,
> Foreknowledge had no influence on their fault.
>
> (3.116-17)

This I emend:

> Foreknowledge had no influence on their *fall.*

The determining repetition is that of the entire passage. Bentley also failed to rescue the following:

> Nor can I think that God, Creator wise,
> Though threatning, will in earnest so destroy
> Us his prime Creatures, dignified so high,
> Set over all his Works, which in our *Fall,*
> For us created, needs with us must faile.
>
> (9.935-42)

Since what happens to man will happen to the works created for him, I amend this to read:

> which in our *Fall,*
> For us created, needs with us must *fall.*

The verbal effect of these passages using the word *fall* may be compared with the following, which is not emended:

> My self and all th' Angelic Host that stand
> In sight of God enthron'd, our happie state
> Hold, as you yours, while our obedience holds;
> on other surety none; freely we serve,
> Because we freely love, as in our will
> To love or not; in this we stand or *fall:*
> And som are *fall'n,* to disobedience *fall'n,*
> And so from Heav'n to deepest Hell; O *fall*
> From what high state of bliss into what woe!
>
> (5.535-43)

Here, as usually, other words enter the iterative pattern: *stand, hold, freely, love. Fall* and *fall'n* are repeated. *Fall* appears at the ends of two lines separated by one ending with *fall'n,* so that identical triple rime is approached. Such use of different forms of the same verb or

48

noun at the ends of consecutive lines is found elsewhere in Milton, as at the beginning of *Paradise Regained:*

> I who e're while the happy Garden sung
> By one mans disobedience lost, now sing
> Recover'd Paradise.

In *Paradise Regained* identical triple rime is once complete, when Satan bewails what he has lost, saying:

> What he bids I do; though I have *lost*
> Much lustre of my native brightness, *lost*
> To be belov'd of God, I have not *lost*
> To love, at least contemplate and admire
> What I see excellent in good, or fair,
> Or vertuous, I should so have *lost* all sense.
>
> (1.577-82)

Here, as usually, the rime word also occurs within a line.

Consider also a passage in *Paradise Regained* dealing with a factual fall, not that of man. Satan, having placed Jesus on a pinnacle of the Temple, where no man by human virtue can stand, expects his victim to fall. But to his astonishment, Jesus, with the words, "Tempt not the lord thy God,"

>   stood.
> But Satan smitten with amazement *fell,*
> As when Earths Son Antaeus (to compare
> Small things with greatest) in Irassa strove
> With Joves Alcides, and oft foil'd still rose,
> Receiving from his mother Earth new strength,
> Fresh from his *fall,* and fiercer grapple joyn'd,
> Throttl'd at length in the air, expir'd and *fell;*
> So after many a foil the Tempter proud,
> Renewing fresh assaults, amidst his pride
> *Fell* whence he stood to see his Victor *fall.*
> And as that Theban Monster that propos'd
> Her riddle, and him, who solv'd it not, devour'd;
> That once found out and solv'd, for grief and spite
> Cast herself headlong from th' Ismenian steep,
> So strook with dread and anguish *fell* the Fiend,
> And to his crew, that sat consulting, brought
> Joyless triumphals of his hop't success,

49

Ruin, and desperation, and dismay,
Who durst so proudly tempt the Son of God.
So Satan *fell*.

(4.561-81)

In these twenty-one lines, various forms of the word *fall* occur seven times, three of them terminal. The passage further demonstrates that my two small but important changes in the Almighty's speech accord with Milton's habits. Such emendation gives to the idea of the Fall of Man the rhetorical and metrical emphasis required by Milton's plan.

Turning to another emendation, I quote from Belial's speech at the council in Hell:

Say they who counsel Warr, we are decreed,
Reserv'd and destin'd to Eternal woe;
Whatever doing, what can we suffer more,
What can we suffer *worse?* is this then *worse,*
Thus sitting, thus consulting, thus in arms?
What when we fled amain, pursu'd and strook
With Heav'ns afflicting Thunder, and besought
The Deep to shelter us? this Hell then seem'd
A refuge from those wounds; or when we lay
Chain'd on the burning Lake? that sure was worse.

(2.160-9)

He continues to imagine further horrors, repeating that their state is not worse than when they were suffering chains and torments, and concluding a line: "This would be *worse*" (186). Then he declares resistance hopeless, saying of their present torments, as he ends another line: "Better these than *worse*" (196). His speech is a refutation of earlier eloquence by Moloch, who imagined the timid, in their hesitation to attack Heaven, as saying:

Should we again provoke
Our stronger, some *worse* way his wrath may find
To our destruction.

Such fears he scorns:

If there be in Hell
Fear to be *worse* destroyed: what can be *worse*

50

> Than to dwell here, driv'n out from Bliss, condemn'd
> In this abhorred deep to utter woe?
>
> (2.82-7)

From this speech by Moloch, with *worse* final in a line, Belial takes his word *worse,* five times repeated, ending four lines (2.163, 169, 186, 196). But in all texts, early and late, Belial is less emphatic, being made to say:

> What can we suffer *worse?* Is this then worst?
>
> (2.163)

That is, the line ends with the superlative *worst,* w-o-r-s-t. To get the effect intended, I emend *worst* to *worse,* thus echoing the word from Moloch, and fitting the series of line endings with which Belial stresses *worse.*

In none of the emendations that I suggest, do I go beyond a single word, sometimes changing only a single letter. Thus I protect myself against Bentley's excesses. Yet I know that all emendation is dangerous. Nevertheless, since I believe that all my changes subserve Milton's intentions, as they accord with his practice, I present them without hesitation, with the hope, indeed with the assurance, that they enhance the effect of the poem for its fit audience.

Duke University (Emeritus)   ALLAN H. GILBERT

Redeeming Time: Milton's
"On the Morning of Christ's Nativity"

IN A CHAPTER ON "The Christian View of History" C. A.
Patrides calls the Nativity Ode "Milton's dress rehearsal for his
performance in *Paradise Lost*." [1] What he is implying, of course, is
that the Nativity Ode foreshadows in its 244 lines some of the major
organizing principles used on a broader scale in *Paradise Lost*. He
is undoubtedly right, especially in regard to the chronological scope
and the Christocentric orientation which his survey of Christian conceptions of time led him to see so clearly in the two poems. In
addition to its affinities with *Paradise Lost,* however, the Nativity
Ode has some unique temporal patterns of its own, and it is the purpose of this paper to examine Milton's use of time in the Ode in its
own right, although with the intention of eventually comparing it
to *Paradise Lost.*

In contrast to *Paradise Lost,* the Nativity Ode is not a narrative, [2]
or at best it is a rudimentary narrative, dependent upon an assumed knowledge of the Nativity story for a contextual matrix. The
poem's cohesiveness is achieved primarily through a complex network of temporal allusions, associated in various ways with the
central event of the child's birth. The organizing scheme, then, is
associative rather than sequential — a feature which helps to explain
the shifting dimensions of time throughout the poem.

These time shifts first appear early in the poem in the relative-
ly simple pattern of the verbs in the opening stanzas. Notice,
for instance, the verbs in the first stanza of the Induction —

---

[1] *Milton and the Christian Tradition* (Oxford, 1966), p. 259.
[2] For a perceptive counterview, See Frank S. Kastor, "Miltonic Narration:
Christ's Nativity," *Anglia,* 86 (1968), 339-352.

inconspicious at first, perhaps, but establishing in their shifting tenses a prelude to the treatment of time in the poem.

> This is the Month, and this the happy morn
> Wherein the Son of Heav'ns eternal King
> Of wedded Maid, and Virgin Mother born,
> Our great redemption from above did bring. [3]

The time established by the first two words, "This *is*," is the poet's time on a particular Christmas morning. It is quickly followed in the next few lines, however, by a rapid flux of past tenses. The shift from present tense, *is,* to the past, *did bring,* may hardly seem worthy of special notice at first, but the shifting tenses become more insistent as the poem proceeds. The immediately following lines read,

> For so the holy sages once did sing,
> That he our deadly forfeit should release,
> And with his Father work us a perpetual peace.

If the holy sages are taken to be the prophets foretelling the coming of the Messiah, the verb "did sing" refers to a time prior to both "did bring" and "is." If the sages are the evangelists telling of Christ after his death, "did sing" refers to a time before "is" but after "did bring." In either case, the verb refers to a different time from that of the first two verbs. The fourth verb, "should release," and the fifth, [should] "work," refer to a time indefinitely in the future from the time of "did sing" — extending, in fact, beyond all subsequent present times to the end of time.

Although these verbs of the opening stanza flow smoothly and cause no particular difficulty in reading, they do move rather rapidly from the opening "is" through several layers of time, creating perhaps some doubt as to which time is to be dominant, or suggesting that the opening present, because of its initial emphasis, is dominant. If doubt *is* raised, however, it is not easily resolved. In fact, it is intensified as the Induction proceeds, particularly in stanzas III and IV. The opening "is" and the emphatic "Now" of line 19 seem to indicate

[3] Merritt Y. Hughes, *John Milton: Complete Poems and Major Prose* (Odyssey Press, 1957), p. 43. All subsequent quotations from the poem are from this edition.

the time of the poet's utterance, dramatically presented as occurring on Christmas morning, 1629, but in stanza IV the poet's time is suddenly merged with the event which he is celebrating. The idea, begun in stanza III, of welcoming the infant God to "his new abode" with the gift of a celebrative poem continues and is developed more fully, but the time becomes ambiguous. Suddenly we see the Magi hasting toward the child with their gifts, and the poet implores his muse to "run" to present her gift first.

> See how from far upon the Eastern road
> The Star-led Wizards haste with odors sweet:
> O run, prevent them with thy humble ode,
> And lay it lowly at his blessed feet;
> Have thou the honor first, thy Lord to greet,
>   And join thy voice unto the Angel Choir,
> From out his secret Altar, toucht with hallow'd fire.

The poet invokes his muse to join her voice — i.e., the poem itself — to the song of the angelic chorus singing on the morning of Christ's birth. The two times merge, at least in the poet's imagination. Christmas morning 1629 and the first Christmas morning are "conflated." [4]

In the four stanzas of the Induction, then, the poet himself becomes a figure within the poem, and his presence creates a point of reference in a complex of shifting times. The perspective established by the poet's time serves as a prelude to the larger dimensions of time which follow, and as the poem develops we realize that those dimensions are indeed large — no less than all time, from creation to Judgment Day.

The fluctuations of tense begun in the Induction continue to appear in the main body of the poem. Stanza I of the section entitled "The Hymn" begins in the past tense, but almost immediately shifts to the present:

> It *was* the Winter wild,
> While the Heav'n-born child,
> All meanly wrapt in the rude manger *lies.*

---

[4] I have appropriated this handy term from Barbara Lewalski's *Milton's Brief Epic,* p. 320.

The Hymn is predominantly in the past tense through the early stanzas, but at recurrent intervals there is a shift to present tense. For instance:

She *woos* the gentle Air	(Stanza II)
Birds of calm *sit* brooding	(V)
The Stars... *stand* fixt	(VI)
The Air... *prolongs* each heav'nly close	(IX)
The helmed Cherubim/And sworded Seraphim/*Are Seen*	(XI)

There are other instances of present tense amid the predominant past tense of the early stanzas, but perhaps these examples will suffice.

I have more to say about the use of tense in the poem, but first I need to talk of another aspect of time in the poem — one that is of even larger import than the shifts of tense, because it provides a context for those shifts. I am thinking of the chronological *scope* of the poem. By that I do not mean the amount of time that elapses from the beginning to the end of the poem, for, since this is hardly a narrative poem, that would be very difficult to compute. Rather I am thinking of the scope of the time references in the poem — the "allusive scope" of the poem, if you will. We have already spoken of the interplay between the first Christmas and Christmas 1629, but that is based on a shifting orientation between two "points" in time, ending in a sudden conflation. I am thinking now, however, of a network of allusions that establishes a chronological context for the poem as a whole. The first such allusion occurs in Stanza XII, where in speaking of the song of the angelic chorus the poet says,

> Such Music (as 'tis said)
> Before was never made,
> But when of old the sons of morning sung,
> While the Creator Great
> His constellations set,
> And the well-balanc't world on hinges hung,
> And cast the dark foundations deep,
> And bid the welt'ring waves their oozy channel keep.

The allusion is of course to the creation — not, however, to the creation as described in the usual Biblical texts such as Genesis or the first verse of John, but as found in Job 38:4-7:

> Where wast thou when I laid the
>   foundations of the earth?
> Declare, if thou hast understanding.
> Who hath laid the measures thereof,
>   if thou knowest?
> Or who hath stretched the line upon
>   it?
> Whereupon are the foundations
>   thereof fastened?
> Or who laid the corner stone thereof;
> when the morning stars sang to-
>   gether
> and all the sons of God shouted for
>   joy?

The obvious reason for the reference to Job rather than, say, Genesis is the presence of celebrative song in the passage in Job. In Milton's poem the joyful song described in Job is remembered and imaginatively blended with the various strands of music and song celebrating the birth of Christ. As the music motif continues, the celestial spheres themselves are called upon to join their "ninefold harmony" to the "Angelic symphony," and the harmony suggested by the blending of the various songs, in turn, initiates a new tense pattern. Stanza XIV begins with a conditional clause which serves as the basis for a series of verbs in what we might call a hypothetical future:

> For if such holy Song
> Enwrap our fancy long,
>   Time *will* run back, and fetch the age of gold,
> And speckl'd vanity
> *Will* sicken soon and die,
>   And leprous sin *will* melt from earthly mold,
> And Hell itself *will* pass away,
> And leave her dolorous mansions to the peering day.

Stanza XV continues in the future tense, culminating in a vision of the future in which,

> Heav'n as at some festival,
> *Will* open wide the Gates of her high Palace Hall.

Then a curious thing happens in regard to the time scheme of the poem. The hypothetical vision of the future is dissolved, and there is a sudden return to the present.

> But wisest Fate says no,
> This must not yet be so;
> The Babe *lies* yet in smiling infancy.

The happy vision proves, like the strewing of the hearse in Lycidas to be a false surmise. But we return to the present and the babe only to veer into the future again, to sterner visions than those momentarily evoked by the harmonious sounds associated with the birth of the child. First we move to the end of the life that is just beginning. The babe lying now in smiling infancy,

> On the bitter cross
> Must redeem our loss;
> So both himself and us to glorify.

Then, in the following lines, there is a movement to the ultimate limits of time:

> Yet first to those chain'd in sleep,
> The wakeful trump of doom must thunder through the deep,
>
> With such a horrid clang
> As on mount Sinai rang
> While the red fire and smold'ring clouds outbrake:
> The aged Earth aghast,
> With terror of that blast,
> Shall from the surface to the center shake,
> When at the world's last session,
> The dreadful Judge in middle Air shall spread his throne.

The sounds in this passage lack the pleasant associations of the previous version of the future. Gabriel's trumpet must thunder through the deep, like the "horrid clang" of the summons at Mount Sinai when Moses spoke with God. The light imagery, too, (red fire and smoldering clouds) suggests power and fear rather than the joyful blend of light and music as in the earlier stanzas, and the passage is full of words like "aghast," "terror," "shake," and "dreadful."

All of this qualifies, I believe, the optimism of the previous vision. The rapture of the "holy Song" on this joyous occasion cannot cause time "to run back, and fetch the age of gold." Christian time begins at the child's birth, but it must move inexorably toward the judgment at the end of time. A new dispensation has begun, but the child himself must die on the bitter cross, and men must continue to struggle in time. The birth is an occasion for joy, certainly. Time now has a new meaning, a new potential. But this potential is not yet fully achieved, and it will not be achieved until the return of Christ as judge at the end of time.

> And *then* at last our bliss
> Full and perfect *is*.
> But *now begins*.

With the emphatically rhyming verb *is*, we return to the present tense, but it is a present placed at the end of time. The vast allusive range of the poem is completed with this simple verb *is*, marking the ultimate limits of future time, and perhaps even intimating an eternal present beyond the limits of time. But if there is a hint of timelessness in this *is*, it is immediately followed by the phrase, "But *now begins*," returning us to the time of the child's birth, where the poem remains, with the exception of three verbs, until the end.

Although the poem remains consistently in the present from this point on, it focuses on the universal impact of the child's birth rather than on the manger scene itself. As Louis Martz remarks, the poem "for most of its course deals with all the world except the manger scene, briefly mentioned in the first stanza, and almost visualized in the last." [5] The emphasis is now on the paradoxical power of the infant, as revealed by the consequences of the birth for the old Dragon of Revelation, and by the flight of the Pagan gods. Only in the final stanza, after the account of the rout of the Pagan deities does the focus return to the time and place where the child lies. And even then the focus is not upon the child but upon the attendant emblems of power:

[5] *The Poetry of Meditation* (Yale, 1962), pp. 164-5.

> But see! the Virgin blest,
> Hath laid her Babe to rest.
>   Time is our tedious Song should here have ending;
> Heav'n's youngest-teemed Star
> Hath fixed her polisht Car,
>   Her sleeping Lord with Handmaid Lamp attending:
> And all about the Courtly Stable,
> Bright-harness'd Angels sit in order serviceable.

The last verb, like the first, is in the present tense, but these final lines depict a moment of stasis. The star is fixed, the child sleeps, and the angels, now seen as armed figures of quiescent power, sit about the courtly stable in bright armor waiting upon their lord. The moment, in the words of Frank Kermode taken from another context, is "purged of simple chronicity." [6] At this node in time, "that which was conceived of as simply successive becomes charged with past and future: What was *chronos* becomes *kairos*." [7]

But even in the poise of this magnificent conclusion, the poet calls attention to the act of composition in which he is engaged, and thereby to his time, when he says,

> Time is our tedious Song should here have ending.

He never lets us completely forget his own point in time. He emphasizes it at strategic points in the poem — particularly at the beginning and the end — using it in conjunction with the fluctuating tense to establish an ambiguous perception of time. Then, after creating ambiguity concerning the present in the early stages of the poem, he establishes through a network of wide ranging allusions a context of total human time within which various presents can be placed. Kenneth Burke's use of the idea of "circumference" seems pertinent here. Burke says,

> When 'defining by location' one may place the object of one's definition in contexts of varying scope. And ... the choice of circumference for the scene in terms of which a given act is to be located will have a corresponding effect upon the interpretation of the act itself. [8]

[6] *The Sense of an Ending* (Oxford University Press, 1967), p. 46.
[7] *Ibid.*
[8] *A Grammar of Motives* (Meridian Books, 1962), p. 77.

And since in the Nativity Ode the circumference is all-inclusive in regard to time, Milton has subsumed into the poem any given moment in time, including — and this is quite important to the effect of the poem — any future time after the dramatized present of the poem's composition on Christmas morning 1629. Once he has established, through his inclusion of the poet's Christmas within the poem, a double reference *in time,* and once he has fully evoked the context of total time, made meaningful by the birth of Christ, he has created a recognition of the possibility within the all-inclusive scope of the poem, of any number of other points in time, all of which can be given coherence by the birth which he is celebrating. Furthermore, since the scope of the poem reaches beyond any particular present, it can include its future readers, and link them all in the vicarious present of the poem's experience. The poem can be revived into imaginative reality by each new reader, and these spots in time may be conflated through their shared experience, both with each other and with the Poet, who has been made the dramatic instrument for building into the poem a consciousness of "other" moments in time, in fact of an almost endless number of such moments. The act of reading is subsumed into the poem. Time is used to defeat time. The theme, as Milton states in Stanza I of the Induction, is "redemption." The poem is a celebration *in time* — and repeatable as it evokes participation from readers in various times — of time as *now* potentially redeeming. [9]

University of North Carolina, Chapel Hill WILLIAM A. McQUEEN

[9] After I had read this paper at the annual meeting of the Southeastern Renaissance Conference, Professor Leigh De Neef called my attention to Lowry Nelson, Jr.'s remarks on "Time as a Means of Structure" in *Baroque Lyric Poetry* (Yale, 1961), pp. 28-84, especially pp. 41-52. Professor Nelson's treatment of the "Nativity Ode" is similar to my own, especially in regard to the poem's tenses, which we both discuss in some detail. Nelson's theory of a biplanar time structure which gradually consolidates into a "new" present is also similar, but not identical, to my idea of multiple times which are unified and given significance by the birth which the poem celebrates. My essay does, I believe, go on to discuss some aspects of time which are only implicit in Nelson's reading, if they are present at all — particularly in my comments on the way the poet functions to involve the reader in the poem and on the relationship of time to the theme of redemption. At any rate, I see the two interpretations as complementary, each confirming the validity of the other and adding different emphases and insights to the core of agreement.